HOW TO
THINK

TACTICAL
THINKING
PUZZLES

For A.E.

Published in 2021 by Welbeck,
an imprint of Welbeck Non-Fiction Limited,
part of Welbeck Publishing Group
20 Mortimer Street, London W1T 3JW

Text and puzzles copyright © 2021 Imagine Puzzles
This edition copyright © 2021 Welbeck Non-Fiction Limited,
part of Welbeck Publishing Group

First published by Eddison Sadd Editions in 2009

A CIP catalogue record for this book is available from the
British Library

ISBN 978-1-78739-784-2

10 9 8 7 6 5 4 3 2 1

Printed in China

TACTICAL
THINKING
PUZZLES

BRAIN-TRAINING PUZZLES TO
HELP YOU SEE THE BIGGER PICTURE

CHARLES PHILLIPS

WELBECK

CONTENTS

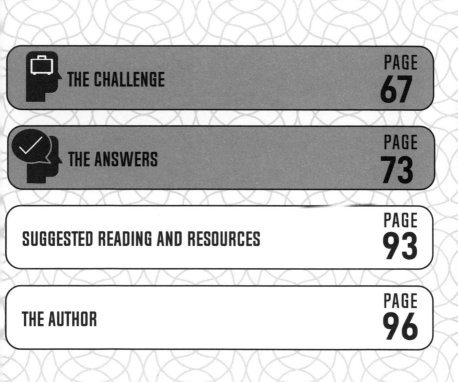

HOW TO THINK TACTICALLY

How do captains of industry achieve success – often against great odds? And how do the top political minds come up with campaigns that manage to catch the spirit of the moment and wrong-foot their opponents?

The answer is that they are good tactical thinkers. They know where they are heading. Even when working under great pressure, dealing with everyday problems, they stay focused on their goals – and so can take advantage of opportunities when these arise. Their thinking is logical and clear, their responses proportionate.

HOW TO BE TACTICAL

This book gives you precious guidance and practise in how to think tactically and strategically like these high achievers. The specially created puzzles, along with the Challenge, are designed to hone your concentration, promote logical reasoning, develop visualization and increase creativity, so you're well positioned to think tactically. Many of the tasks require you to hold a number of future possibilities in view – like a game of chess – while considering the effects of particular moves. They have been chosen to develop the skills you need to think for tactical thinking.

THE WOOD AND THE TREES

Tactical thinking enables you to be prepared, to stay one step ahead of your opponents and your problems. To do this, you need to be absorbed in the task at hand and on what is coming next, and, crucially, to see how both fit into your long-term plan. As well as being task-focused, you must always be goal-oriented. You need to be alert while performing a task, but also to take the long view and remember your aims. You have to plan your time, use your resources efficiently and ensure that you work as effectively as you can.

The key first step is to get perspective. If you are stuck dealing with immediate problems you cannot get an overview. What are you aiming for? Check that what you are doing is really useful in terms of your goal. In other words, you need to be able to see the wood as well as the trees.

TACTICAL OR STRATEGIC?

Business and management books distinguish between operational, tactical and strategic thinking. Operational thinking covers day-to-day operations, work in the office or on the shop floor. Tactical thinking is medium-term, say, for a six- or 12-month period, and strategic thinking is long-term. In this terminology, tactical thinking is subordinate to strategic thinking. A manager determines a strategy, then chooses tactics to put the strategy into effect.

For our purposes, we need to consider both tactical and strategic approaches. Both are key weapons in your armoury if you're to take an intelligent approach to meeting challenges and solving problems.

PRESENTATION AND CREATIVITY

Tactical performance requires good presentation. You need to know what to say and to say it well. You require clear logic and good debating skills. And sometimes you need the ability to see an unexpected move, to "think outside the box".

DON'T RUSH IN!

Don't forget, though, that a tactical response is a realistic one. To be tactical, as we have seen, you need to keep your goal in mind and plan what you are going to say and do. You have to teach yourself, therefore, not to rush in. Consider before you speak.

THINK OF A BRIGHTER FUTURE

Tactical thinking may initially seem like something you do at work—managing problems, setting goals, meeting targets. But it's a thinking skill you need in every part of your life. When you think tactically, you are planning the path best designed to reach any goal you have in mind. Tactical skills of the kind developed in this book are what you need to shape your planning and think your way to a brighter future. So let's get started. Turn the page, focus and learn to think tactically ...

INTRODUCTION

THE PUZZLES IN THIS BOOK

There are three levels of puzzles to work through, each with a "time to beat" deadline. These deadlines apply a little pressure – we often think better when we set ourselves goals such as time constraints. But don't worry about these limits – they are no more than guidelines. So if you find that you are taking longer than the "ideal" time, relax. Look out for puzzles marked Time Plus. You'll almost certainly need a bit longer to complete these – not because they are more difficult, but because there's more work to do to solve them.

Some puzzles have another similar version later in the book, to give you even more practise. Where we feel you might need some help, a tip has been provided, and there are Notes and Scribbles pages at the back of the book. Also towards the end of the book, the Challenge is designed to give your newly acquired tactical-thinking skills a thorough workout. With a suggested time limit of 10–15 minutes, you have a chance to consider and reconsider a series of problems, to marshal available resources and plot a response, perhaps make a few notes and try out ideas in the margin space provided.

You'll find as your new skills develop that you'll become better able to adapt your plans according to pressing circumstances so that you achieve your goals, demonstrating to yourself and others that you are a resourceful and tactical thinker. So, look sharpish and let's get started!

PUZZLE GRADING	TIME TO BEAT
EASY = WARM-UP	1–2 MINUTES
MEDIUM = WORKOUT	3–4 MINUTES
DIFFICULT = WORK HARDER	5–6 MINUTES
TIME-PLUS PUZZLES	6+ MINUTES
THE CHALLENGE	10–15 MINUTES

50
PUZZLES
FOR
TACTICAL
THINKING

REMEMBER. Take it step by step. But keep your eyes on the goal. Stay focused to think **TACTICALLY**

EASY PUZZLES
FOR LATERAL THINKING

The puzzles and challenges in this first section of the book give your tactical-thinking skills a warm-up. They're designed to develop your concentration, while giving you practise in visualization and plotting connections in a sequence. This section includes exercises that call for prediction skills, and these are good for overall thinking because they really get your brain cells firing.

PUZZLE 1
SYMBOL SIMON

Games developer Simon created this simple symbol game for a handheld electronic computer device. The screen displays a pattern of symbols within a grid, with number totals given – as shown below. Each symbol stands for a different number. In order to reach the correct total at the end of each row and column, a player must work out the value of the circle, cross, pentagon, square and star. Simon gives it to his friend Piper to test. Can you help her solve the symbol code?

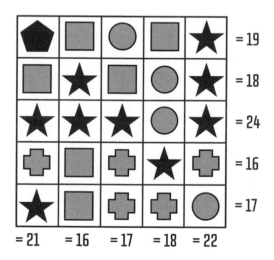

HOW TO
THINK
TIP

Try starting with the third row down or the far-right column to work out the value of a star.

12

PUZZLE 2
GIOVANNI'S ICE CREAM PUZZLE

Cafe owner Giovanni devised a "Birthday Special" consisting of scoops of ice cream each marked with a chocolate letter to spell the name of the person celebrating his or her birthday. Then, at a party for mathematics teacher Noah, he created a puzzle, as shown below.

The letters are valued 1–26 according to their places in the alphabet. Can you help Noah crack the mystery code to reveal the missing letter in the fifth dessert?

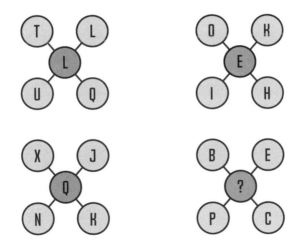

HOW TO **THINK** TIP

After converting the letters into numbers, how do you get to the central number? In the first dessert, for example, what's the relationship between the central number and the other four?

PUZZLE 3
NUMBERCLUSE

Adrian embeds this Numbercluse game into a detective novel he is writing in which the hero, Arthur, is a maths professor turned private investigator. Arthur finds several clues and has to place the correct answers in the grid. Can you help him? All are whole numbers, no two are the same, none has a value of less than one or more than 63, and two numbers have been placed to get you started.

1 A1 is either C2 plus C3 or C2 minus C3
2 A2 is A1 plus D2
3 A3 is C3 divided by B2
4 A4 is either A3 plus B3 or B2 plus B3
5 B1 is either A2 plus C1 or A2 minus C1
6 B2 is one third of C3 7 B3 is C3 plus D4
8 B4 is either A4 minus A3 or A4 minus D4
9 C1 is one third of A4
10 C2 is B4 plus C1
11 C3 is either 11 or 12
12 C4 is A1 divided by A3

13 D1 is B2 plus C3
14 D2 is either C4 plus D3 or C4 minus D3
15 D3 is one third of C1
16 D4 is A3 multiplied by D1.

	1	2	3	4	
					A
					B
			12		C
			7		D

**HOW TO
THINK
TIP**

I find it can help to draw a diagram showing relations between the numbers in this kind of puzzle.

PUZZLE 4
GRANDPA WILSON'S BATTLESHIP

Grandpa Wilson, a retired history teacher, has devised his own version of the well-known paper-and-pencil game of battleship. In his game, the numbers on the side and bottom of the grid indicate occupied squares or groups of consecutive occupied squares in each row or column. He gives the game to his twin grandsons, Nile and Nathan, to play, telling them, "You have to fill up the grid in such a way that it contains three cruisers, three launches and three buoys – but you must ensure that the numbers make sense."

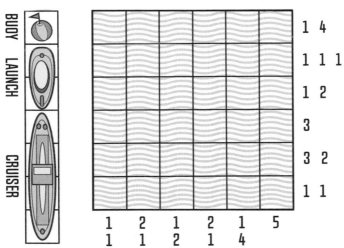

Looking at the far-left column and the top row, you can tell that the top-left square must be occupied by a buoy.

PUZZLE 5
MATHS MOB T-SHIRT

Inspirational teacher Mr. Goldstein holds an after-school mathematics club he calls "Maths Mob". He designs a number grid (as below) to put on a special T-shirt for members. Then at the last minute he decides to block out some numbers so there are no duplicates in rows or columns.

He phones the printer, Hasan, to tell him. He says, "Please block out some numbers so that there are no duplicates in any row or column. OK? But connections are important, too: Blocked-out (black) cells may not touch along a straight line either horizontally or vertically (although they can touch at a corner) and the other (unblocked) squares must be connected horizontally and/or vertically." Can you help Hasan?

4	3	4	2	5	4
2	1	3	1	4	2
4	5	1	4	3	2
4	2	1	5	1	5
5	4	2	1	4	3
1	1	4	3	2	5

HOW TO THINK TIP

The top line looks simple enough as a starting point.

PUZZLE 6
NUMBERCROSS

In this ingenious number crossword, every row and column contains the same numbers and mathematical signs, but they are arranged in a different order each time. Can you find the correct order to arrive at the totals shown, both horizontally and vertically?

4	x	2	−	6	+	1	=	3
							=	26
							=	30
							=	10
=		=		=		=		
12		4		6		14		

HOW TO THINK TIP

Before trying to enter any numbers in the grid, note down the ways in which 4, 2, 6 and 1 can be combined using x, − and + to produce the required number totals.

PUZZLE 7
BALLOON MOVE

Four balloons, two green and two black, have numbers printed on them, as shown. The row of balloons is rearranged. Can you work out the new sequence from the clues that follow:

1 The odd numbers are next to each other.
2 So too are the green balloons.
3 The extreme left-hand number is worth twice the one next to it.

HOW TO THINK TIP

Can you start with clue 3?

18

WARM-UP

1-2
MINUTES

PUZZLE 8
ELLIOTT'S NUMBER GRID

Physics students Elliott and Morris took jobs as security guards to pay some bills. Work was slow one day and Elliott devised this number-grid game using the back of coupons. He told Morris, "Place the eight coupons into the puzzle grid so that all of the adjacent numbers on each coupon match up. Coupons may be rotated, but none may be flipped over." Can you help Morris complete the number grid?

HOW TO THINK TIP

Try starting with the bottom-left coupon.

PUZZLE 9
THE MATHS HOUSE

Vikram finds this puzzle on Level 1 of his educational video game "The Maths House." He enters a room with a 4 x 4 grid, as shown, on the floor. To pass across he must fill the grid with the numbers 4, 6, 7, 7, 8, 8, 10, 10, 10, 10, 10, 11, 12, 12, 13 and 14 so that each line across, down and diagonally adds up to 38. How should he fill up the grid?

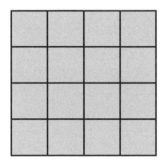

 **HOW TO THINK TIP**

Will it help to list the different combinations of these numbers that add up to 38? Remember – there are pages provided for Notes and Scribbles at the back of the book.

PUZZLE 10
MR AWESOME'S DEBTS

Mr Awesome (A) owes £50 to Ms Brilliant (B), while Mrs Dreamy (D) owes
Mr Charming (C) £40, and so on for the other transactions shown below.
How can these five debts be settled by two simple repayments?

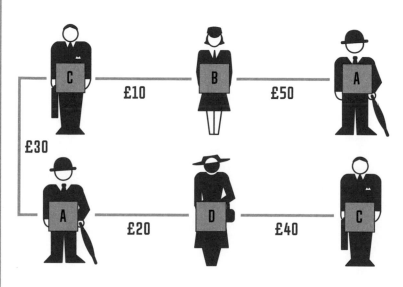

HOW TO THINK TIP

Work out the amounts owing and owed for each character.

21

PUZZLE 11
HEXAGON HAVEN

Designer Emmanuel created this hexagon number game for his nephews Jorge and Diego. He instructed them to place the hexagons into the central grid so that where one touches another along a bold line the contents of both triangles are the same, and he insisted that no rotation of any hexagon is allowed. Can you help the boys?

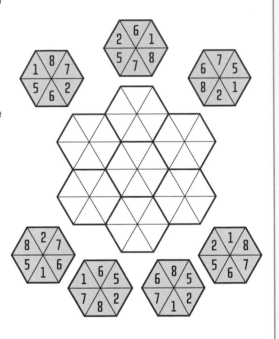

HOW TO THINK TIP

Be prepared for a certain amount of trial and error. But here's a tip to get you going – the bottom triangle in the grid should contain a 1.

PUZZLE 12
L-O

Philosophy teacher Ella devised the L-O game as a test of perception, logic and tactical thinking for her students. There are 12 L-shapes, three of each of the four kinds shown here. Each L has one O-shaped hole in it, and they have been inserted in the grid. Given the positions of the Os in the diagram, can you tell where the Ls must be?

Any piece may be turned or flipped over before being put in the grid. No pieces of the same kind may touch, even at a corner. The pieces fit together so well that you cannot see any spaces between them; only the holes show.

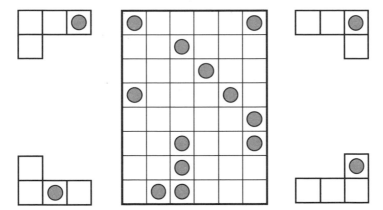

HOW TO
THINK
TIP

The two Ls across the top both face the same way.

PUZZLE 13
CAP STARS

Do you like the designs artist Jerome made for printing on rugby caps? He's very strict about presenting them in a logical pattern on his market stall. But today he's sick and his brother Edwin has to get the pattern right in his absence. Which of the four boxed designs should Edwin use to complete the pattern and fill the space?

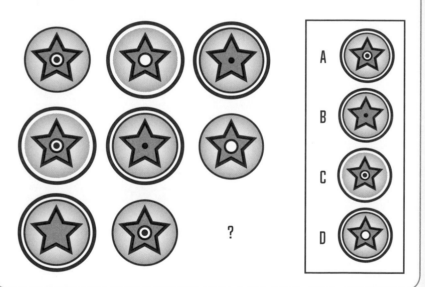

 **HOW TO THINK TIP**

Don't overlook the detailing on the circle enclosing the star.

24

PUZZLE 14
NUMBER CONNECT

Numbers really connect in this grid. Can you fit all of the listed numbers into the crossword-style layout? One number is given to help you get started.

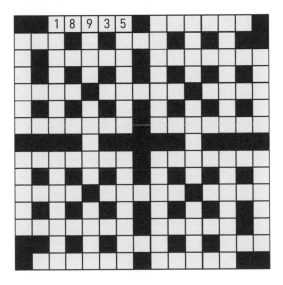

3 digits	4876	43703	462479	5521411
128	5033	55662	736724	5539957
247	7262	63058	815256	6701014
592	8124	74906		7012450
659	9368	76149	**7 digits**	7368351
		80231	1759236	8297012
4 digits	**5 digits**	91427	2034719	8827064
1951	~~18935~~		3403834	9638357
2407	22514	**6 digits**	3532382	9748536
3915	31970	290857	4374193	

25

PUZZLE 15
GENERAL DRAG'S ACADEMY

General Drag makes the cadets at his military academy develop their tactical nous with this exercise. The General gives them the plan shown below of a camping ground dotted with trees and tells them to add tents according to the following rules. Each tent must be either immediately above, below or beside its tree. No two tents can be on adjacent squares (even diagonally). The numbers at the end of each row and column indicate how many tents they must contain. Have a go yourself to see how well you'd do at the academy.

HOW TO
THINK
TIP

Start with the bottom two rows of the grid.

26

PUZZLE 16
MEL'S CHESS CHALLENGE

Pals Mel and Marvin love to play chess at "The Old Barber Shop" cafe. When they're not playing matches, they set each other challenges, and here's one Mel set Marvin. How can the knight land on all of the remaining eleven squares on this section of the board using eleven standard knight's moves? What would you do if you were Marvin?

HOW TO THINK TIP

Remember: a knight makes an L-shaped move – either two squares horizontally and one square vertically, or two squares vertically and one square horizontally.

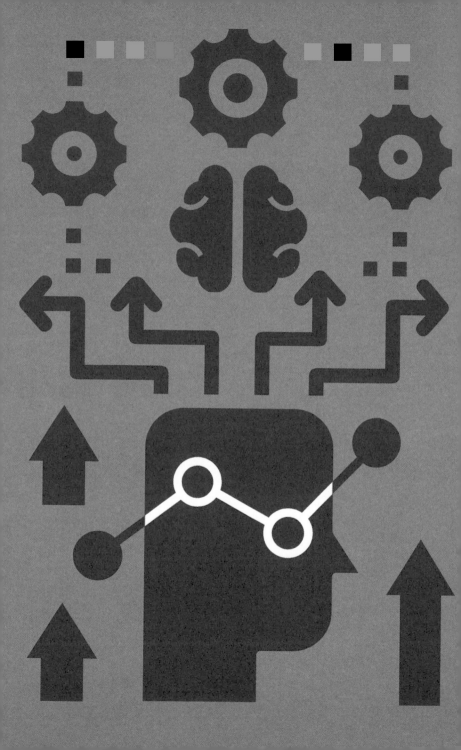

MEDIUM PUZZLES

FOR LOGICAL THINKING

In this section we move on to medium-difficulty puzzles and tests to give your developing powers of tactical thinking some more demanding practice. The visual, numerical and language puzzles here call on you to make a calculated response. Be shrewd. Look for connections and patterns. If you find any of the puzzles very difficult, take a break. Scientists tell us that we are likely to think best when we are engaged and interested.

PUZZLE 17
SAM'S SUDOKU

Sam devised and drew a set of sudokus as a present for his puzzle-mad girlfriend, Grace. Can you help Grace fill in the empty squares so that each 3 x 3 block of nine and each vertical and horizontal line contains all of the numbers from 1 to 9?

6				5	7	4	9	
				9		5		6
	9	5						
							4	2
	5		4		6		8	
8	3							
						1	2	
9		3		1				
	1	2	7	8				3

HOW TO THINK TIP

Start where you see the most numbers.

30

PUZZLE 18
ALPHABET XPLORER

Femi encounters this tactical challenge playing a game called "Alphabet Xplorer" on his new mobile phone. His heart sinks because geography is not his strong point. Can you help him? Each oval shape should contain a different letter from A to K inclusive. Use the clues to determine the locations of the letters. (When the clues refer to "due", they mean in any location along the same horizontal or vertical line.)

1 B is due west of A, which is next to and due north of J.
2 E is further east than D.
3 G is due north of E and due west of C.
4 I is next to and due north of H, which is further north than both F and C.
5 K is due north of D and due west of F.

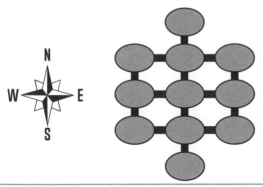

HOW TO
THINK
TIP

Use a pencil to try out combinations of letters, or copy the grid onto the Notes and Scribbles pages and test your theories there.

PUZZLE 19
GRANDPA WILSON'S BATTLESHIP 2

Here's another battleship game that Grandpa Wilson drew for young Nile and Nathan (see Puzzle 4). As before, the numbers on the side and below the grid indicate occupied squares or groups of consecutive occupied squares in each row or column. The task for the boys is to fill up the grid so that it contains three cruisers, three launches and three buoys, and to ensure that all of the numbers make sense. Can you help them?

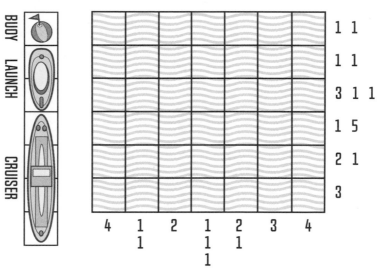

HOW TO THINK TIP

Start with either of the two end columns, which look like they may each contain a cruiser.

PUZZLE 20
DOMZONE

Lloyd writes this puzzle for his domino games website, Domzone. A standard set of 28 dominoes is laid out as shown below. Players have to draw in the edges of them all using the computer mouse. How will you fare on our paper version? The tick box is provided as an aid; one domino has already been placed, as shown.

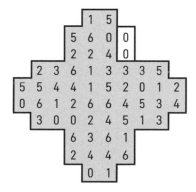

0-0	0-1	0-2	0-3	0-4	0-5	0-6
✓						

1-1	1-2	1-3	1-4	1-5	1-6	2-2

2-3	2-4	2-5	2-6	3-3	3-4	3-5

3-6	4-4	4-5	4-6	5-5	5-6	6-6

HOW TO THINK TIP

Are the doubles the best dominoes to start with?

33

PUZZLE 21
SYMBOL TRANSFER

Each row and column in this grid originally contained one circle, one diamond, one square, one triangle and two blank squares, although not necessarily in that order. Every symbol with a green arrow refers to the first of the four symbols encountered when travelling in the direction of the arrow. Every symbol with a white arrow refers to the second of the four symbols encountered in the direction of the arrow. Can you complete the original grid?

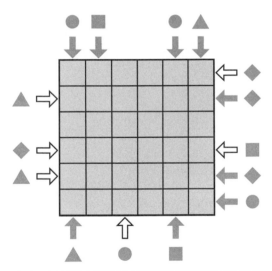

HOW TO THINK TIP

The circle in the first column doesn't travel far.

34

PUZZLE 22
GRIDBLOCK

Can you place all 12 gridblock pieces in the grid? Any piece may be rotated or flipped over but may touch another, not even diagonally. The numbers refer to the number of consecutive black squares from left to right or top to bottom; each block is separated from the others by at least one white square. So, 3, 2 could refer to a row with none, one or more white squares, then three black squares, at least one white square, two black squares, followed by any number of white squares.

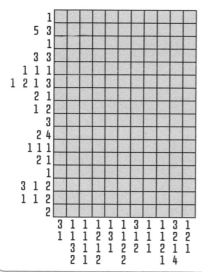

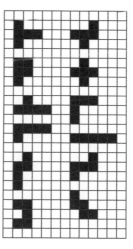

35

PUZZLE 23
THE MATHS HOUSE 2

Vikram finds another, slightly harder version of the number grid as he progresses to level two of his game "The Maths House" (see Puzzle 9). This time he finds himself in a desert, and to cross the shifting sands he must fill the grid with the numbers 5, 6, 8, 9, 9, 10, 11, 11, 12, 13, 13, 13, 14, 16, 18 and 20 in such a way that each line across, down and diagonally adds up to 47.

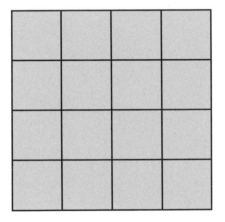

HOW TO
THINK
TIP

11 + 11 + 12 + 13 is one way of making 47. Is it worth noting down the others before attempting to fill in the grid?

PUZZLE 24
WHAT'S IN JEM'S BOX?

Maths professor Mrs Jay adopted seven sons and named them Jim, Joe, Jack, Jeff, Jordan, Jamal and Jem. Can you crack the code below to uncover a hidden sequence that will reveal the value of Jem's box?

STEP 1: Examine the horizontal lines already positioned in the boys' boxes on the bottom row and match them with those marked A–H on the top row by a process of elimination. For example, only one of the A–H boxes may have three horizontal lines, etc.

STEP 2: Once you have deduced which lettered box matches a boy's box (based on the horizontals), fill in all the diagonals and vertical lines on the box as a double-check. A box must have a diagonal (running either way) if it has a green circle at its centre.

STEP 3: As you deduce which lettered box matches which boy's box, write down the value of each boy's box (for example, box C = 17).

STEP 4: When you've uncovered the values of all of the boys' boxes, work out the hidden number sequence, then you'll be able to work out the value of Jem's box.

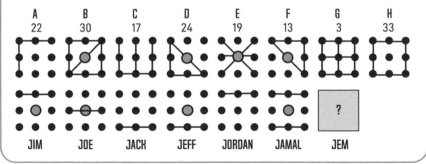

A	B	C	D	E	F	G	H
22	30	17	24	19	13	3	33

JIM   JOE   JACK   JEFF   JORDAN   JAMAL   JEM

HOW TO
THINK
TIP

The only horizontal on both Jim and Jordan's boxes is at the top, so these must match shapes A and F. But note that only one of A and F has a diagonal.

37

PUZZLE 25
CRISTIANO'S COUNTER FLIP

Medical student Cristiano Solo devised this counter flip during a holiday job selling ice creams. Each of the nine counters has a green and a white face. One move consists of flipping over a counter and all the counters directly touching it – marked with an X in the examples. Which three moves should you use to turn all of these counters so that they show the green side up?

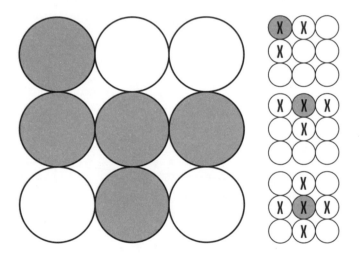

PUZZLE 26
NUMBERCROSS 2

Here's another, more challenging, number crossword (see Puzzle 6), in which each row and column contains the same numbers and mathematical signs, but they are arranged in a different order every time. Can you find the correct order to arrive at the totals shown, both horizontally and vertically?

9	−	5	x	7	+	8	=	36
	■		■		■			
							=	54
	■		■		■			
							=	42
	■		■		■			
							=	52
=	■	=	■	=	■	=		
74		34		25		50		

HOW TO THINK TIP

Does it help to work backwards from the totals – for example, by trying to divide 50 by 5, then playing around with the other numbers?

PUZZLE 27
SQUARE DANCE

These four squares have been rearranged. Can you work out the new sequence from the clues that follow?

1 The square containing a star no longer shares a vertical side with the square with a triangle.
2 One of the squares has not moved.
3 The square containing the star is now in the top row.
4 The star remains further right than the circle.

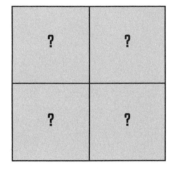

HOW TO THINK TIP

Start by moving the square containing a star.

PUZZLE 28
OLGA'S BIRTHDAY CHALLENGE

After they turned 60, Boris and Olga developed an interesting family tradition. Instead of a present, each birthday Boris gives Olga a puzzle – and vice versa. This number-and-symbol network is the puzzle Olga devises for Boris's 70th. Can you help him solve it? The rules are as follows. Every square in the grid must contain one number and one shape. Each horizontal row and vertical column should contain different shapes and different numbers. No combination of number and shape may be repeated anywhere in the puzzle.

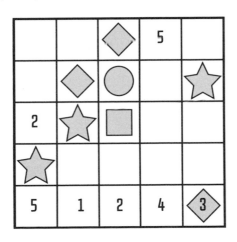

 **HOW TO THINK TIP**

Perhaps the best tactic is to solve the alignment of shapes before attempting to put the numbers in place?

41

PUZZLE 29

MORRIS'S NUMBER GRID

Morris enjoyed solving his friend Elliott's number grid (see Puzzle 8) and devised a slightly harder one for his friend to do when he was working a late shift as a security guard. As before, the rules are place the eight coupons into the puzzle grid so that all adjacent numbers on each coupon match up; coupons may be rotated, but none may be flipped over.

4	3
1	1

2	2
4	4

4	2
2	4

1	2
4	4

2	3
3	1

4	4
3	4

3	2
1	4

4	2
1	3

				4	2
				3	2

HOW TO THINK TIP

The top-left and bottom-right squares contain the same number.

PUZZLE 30
GENERAL DRAG'S ACADEMY 2

The cadets at General Drag's Academy (see Puzzle 15) failed to keep their barracks tidy, so the general got them up at 06.00 for a gruelling run followed by this tactical-thinking test. As before, the general gives the cadets the plan shown below of a camping ground dotted with trees and tells them to add tents according to the following rules.

Next to every tree you must draw a tent. Each tent must either be immediately above, below or beside its tree, and no two tents can be on adjacent squares (even diagonally). The numbers at the end of each row and column tell you how many tents they must contain. Can you help the cadets satisfy the General?

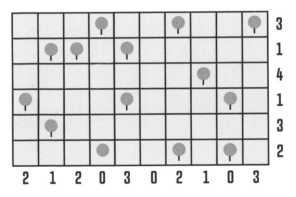

HOW TO THINK TIP

Try starting where there are no tents.

43

PUZZLE 31
NUMBER CONNECT 2

Here's another of our Number Connect puzzles (see Puzzle 14). Can you fit these numbers into the grid? As before, one number is given to get you started.

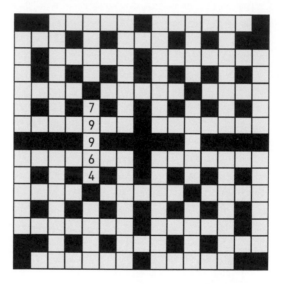

3 digits	4157	38426	412237	3491267
745	6209	42615	709825	4077202
764	6918	53027	780735	4383619
817	7522	61463		5073587
870	7553	79964	**7 digits**	5571903
		86538	1230872	6832343
4 digits	**5 digits**	98533	1263207	7816591
1574	14552		2123871	8618730
1965	25361	**6 digits**	2313852	9265786
2815	26839	405496	3350958	

44

PUZZLE 32
GREGORY'S CARDTHINK

Gregory devises logical posers that he calls "cardthinks" for his friends at the Bridgetown Bridge Club. Here's one he created for his friend Anton. Can you help him solve it? Gregory asks, "What is the face value and suit of each of the cards shown? Together they total 81. All 12 cards used are of different values. In the pack, the value of the cards are as per their numbers, and Ace = 1, Jack = 11, Queen = 12 and King = 13. No card is horizontally or vertically next to another of the same colour, and there are four different suits in each horizontal row and three different suits in each vertical column.

1. The 4 of Diamonds is directly next to and right of the 7, which is directly next to and below the 5, which is of a different suit to the 8.
2. The Queen of Spades is directly next to and above the King, which is directly next to and right of the Ace .
3. Card F has a value three lower than that of card H. Card B has a value two higher than that of card G.
4. The Jack of Clubs is directly next to (either horizontally or vertically) the 2."

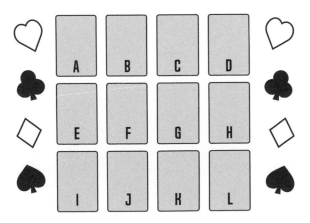

45

PUZZLE 33
DOMZONE DRINKS TRAY

Domino-mad puzzler Lloyd made this metal drinks tray to promote his games website Domzone (see Puzzle 20). The tray is covered with symbols as shown below and comes with magnetic domino outlines. The task is to divide the symbols up into domino shapes (each containing two symbols) so that none of the resulting ten dominoes is like any of the others in the set – each is unique.

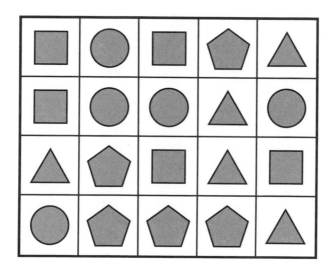

Consider whether identical symbols should be kept together or kept apart when making the dominoes.

46

PUZZLE 34
SYMBOL SIMON 2

Here's another of the symbol games that Simon developed for his handheld
computer game (see Puzzle 1). As before, each symbol stands for a different
number. In order to reach the correct total at the end of each row and column,
what is the value of the circle, cross, pentagon, square and star?

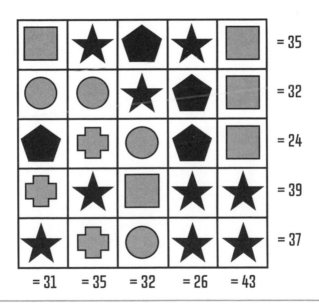

HOW TO THINK TIP

Try copying the grid, drawing the symbols smaller
and pencilling in possible values for the symbols.

DIFFICULT PUZZLES
FOR TACTICAL THINKING

 WORK HARDER   **5-6** MINUTES

You'll have to work harder to solve the puzzles in this third part of the book, which contains the most demanding of our exercises in tactical thinking. These challenges require close attention and an ability to think through a sequence while maintaining a sense of perspective. Keep the aim of every task in mind and be aware that you may sometimes need to call on your creativity and intuition. Remember that the exercises are intended to be enjoyable. You'll learn more quickly, and come to be a better tactical thinker in the end, if you're able to stay positive. Have fun!

WORK HARDER

5-6
MINUTES

PUZZLE 35
SYMBOL TRANSFER 2

This is a second chance to try your hand at one of our Symbol Transfer puzzles (see Puzzle 21). As before, each row and column in this grid originally contained one circle, one diamond, one square, one triangle and two blank squares, although not necessarily in that order. Every symbol with a green arrow refers to the first of the four symbols encountered when travelling in the direction of the arrow. Every symbol with a white arrow refers to the second of the four symbols encountered in the direction of the arrow. Can you complete the original grid?

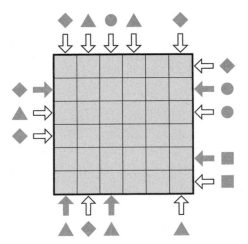

The triangle at the bottom left makes only a short journey.

50

PUZZLE 36
NUMBERCLUSE 2

Adrian's novel about Arthur, the mathematics prof turned private investigator (see Puzzle 3), is a big hit, and for the movie adaptation the screenwriter asks him to come up with a second, more difficult Numbercluse puzzle. Can you help Arthur discover the 16 numbers that match all the "cluse" below? All are whole numbers, no two are the same and none has a value of less than one.

1 A1 is B3 minus B1

2 A2 is C2 plus D1

3 A3 is B1 divided by D3

4 A4 is either D4 minus B4 or D4 divided by D3

5 B1 is either C4 plus 12 or C4 minus 12

6 B2 is A4 divided by A3

7 B3 is D4 minus C4

8 B4 is either half or double A1

9 C1 is B2 multiplied by D3

10 C2 is D1 plus C4

11 C3 is either D2 minus A2 or D2 minus B3

12 C4 is either 16 or 17

13 D1 is either C4 divided by D3 or C4 plus D3

14 D2 is either B4 plus C1 or B4 minus C1

15 D3 is one quarter of C4

16 D4 is either A2 plus B1 or A2 minus B1

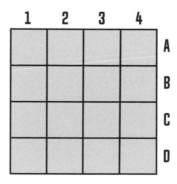

PUZZLE 37
SAM'S SUDOKU 2

Grace enjoyed the sudoku that Sam made for her (see Puzzle 17). So on her birthday Sam drew another slightly harder version of the puzzle. Can you help Grace fill in the empty squares so that each 3 x 3 block of nine, and each vertical and horizontal line contains all of the numbers from 1 to 9?

4						1		9
		1			5		3	6
			1				4	
		9		2	3			7
			8		9			
8			6	5		2		
	6				7			
2	8		5			9		
9		7						5

Competition adds spice and sometimes improves thinking performance. Why not copy the sudoku quickly by hand and then do it against a friend or family member?

52

PUZZLE 38
GRIDBLOCK 2

Try your hand at another Gridblock (see Puzzle 22), placing all 12 pieces in the grid. Any piece may be rotated or flipped over, but none may touch another, not even diagonally. The numbers outside the grid refer to the number of consecutive black squares from left to right or top to bottom, and each block is separated from the others by at least one white square. For instance, 3, 2 could refer to a row with none, one or more white squares, then three black squares, at least one white square, two more black squares, followed by any number of white squares.

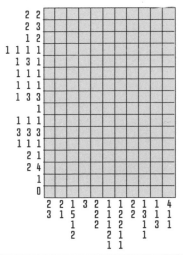

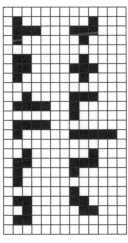

You could start with the five consecutive squares in the third column.

53

PUZZLE 39
HEXAGON HAVEN 2

Emmanuel's nephews Jorge and Diego enjoyed their uncle's hexagon number game (see Puzzle 11) and asked for another for their birthday present. This is what he came up with – can you help them? As before, the task is to place the hexagons into the central grid, so that where one touches another along a straight line, the contents of both triangles are the same. No rotation of any hexagon is allowed.

HOW TO THINK TIP

The best way to approach this puzzle may be to treat it as a game of chance.

PUZZLE 40
WHAT'S IN BELLE'S BOX ?

Philosophy teacher Mr Bee has a similar problem as his friend Mrs Jay (see
Puzzle 24). Mr Bee has adopted seven daughters: Bea, Bliss, Bess, Beth,
Buffy, Bunty and Belle. Can you crack the code to uncover the hidden number
sequence that will reveal the value of Belle's box?

STEP 1: Examine the horizontal lines already positioned in the girls' boxes in
the bottom row and match them with those marked A–H in the top row by a
process of elimination. For example, only one of the A–H boxes may have three
horizontal lines, etc.

STEP 2: Once you have deduced which lettered box matches a girl's box (based
on the horizontals), fill in all the diagonals and vertical lines on the girl's box as
a double-check. A box must have a diagonal (running right–left or left–right) if
it has a green circle at its center.

STEP 3: As you deduce which lettered box matches which girl's box, write down
the value of each girl's box (for example, box C = 17).

STEP 4: When you've uncovered the values of all of the girls' boxes, work out the
hidden number sequence.

STEP 5: Once you've cracked the sequence, you'll be able to work out the value
of Belle's box.

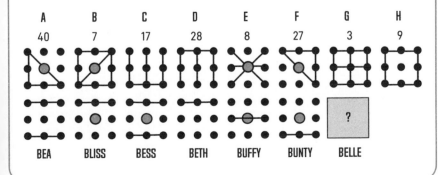

55

PUZZLE 41
TURN 2 CONNECT

Chaim developed Turn 2 Connect as a machine-age version of a simple old-fashioned game like Solitaire. The task is to rotate each of these discs using multiples of 90-degree turns only, so that all the squares are connected by the network of horizontal and vertical lines.

To help you with this paper version of Chaim's game, we have provided a blank grid alongside.

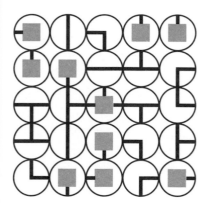
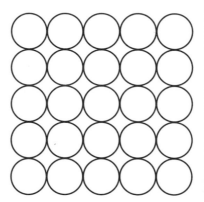

HOW TO
THINK
TIP

Remember that if you find that you are stuck on this, or any puzzle, try taking a break. Go for a walk, make yourself a hot drink, rest your eyes by looking out of the window. You're allowed to "stop the clock" on the puzzle's time limit.

PUZZLE 42
GIOVANNI'S SECOND ICE CREAM PUZZLE

Noah enjoys the ice cream code-breaker set by cafe owner Giovanni (see Puzzle 2) and asks him to make another for his girlfriend, Rebecca. As before, the letters are valued 1–26 according to their places in the alphabet. Rebecca has to crack the mystery code to reveal the missing letter. Can you help her?

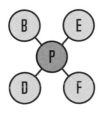

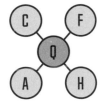

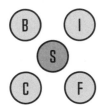

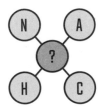

Think about whether you've managed to take away any new knowledge from previous puzzles about pattern recognition.

PUZZLE 43
BORIS'S BIRTHDAY CHALLENGE

Boris is very pleased with the puzzle that Olga devises for his 70th birthday (see Puzzle 28). He resolves to make one of the same kind for Olga when she turns 70, and this is the puzzle he creates.

As before, each horizontal row and vertical column should contain different shapes and different numbers; every square will contain one number and one shape and no combination may be repeated anywhere else in the puzzle.

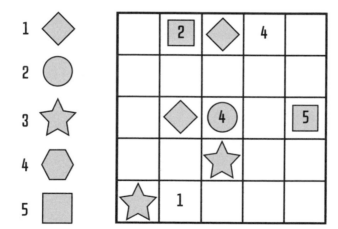

The bottom-left and top-right squares contain matching shapes.

PUZZLE 44
GREGORY'S CARDTHINK 2

Here's another of the "cardthink" puzzles that Gregory devises for his friends at the Bridgetown Bridge Club (see Puzzle 32). As before, you have to work out the face value and suit of each card shown.

Together they total 85. All 12 cards used are of different values. In the pack, the value of the cards are as per their numbers, and Ace = 1, Jack = 11, Queen = 12 and King = 13. No card is horizontally or vertically next to another of the same colour, and there are four different suits in each horizontal row and three different suits in each vertical column.

1 Card C has a value two lower than that of card G, which is a Heart. Card J has a higher value than that of card D.
2 The 5 is directly next to and above the King, which is directly next to and right of the Jack.
3 The 7 is directly next to and left of the Queen of Diamonds, which is directly next to and above the 3 of Spades.
4 The 8 is directly next to and above the 9 of Spades.

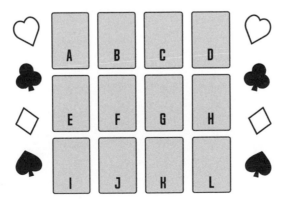

59

PUZZLE 45
MATHS MOB MOUSE MAT

Mr Goldstein's Maths Mob mathematics club (see Puzzle 5) is going from strength to strength, and he wants to get a mouse mat printed for members. He sends the layout of numbers to the printer, Hasan, but it gets separated from its overlay, which marks some numbers to be blocked out.

As before, Mr Goldstein calls Hasan and tells him, "Please block out numbers so that there are no duplicates in any row or column. But remember about connections, too: Blocked-out (black) cells may not touch along a straight line either horizontally or vertically (although they can touch at a corner) and the other (unblocked) squares must be connected horizontally and/or vertically." Can you help Hasan?

1	7	2	9	4	3	2	3	6	8
1	2	7	8	4	9	1	1	9	4
3	8	2	8	5	7	1	4	9	6
6	9	7	2	5	5	7	8	3	3
4	9	5	3	6	1	4	7	8	9
6	4	6	1	5	2	8	1	5	4
8	6	1	5	7	4	4	6	3	5
9	5	4	6	2	8	2	3	1	7
5	8	8	9	9	2	6	2	1	1
5	6	3	5	4	4	9	7	7	2

HOW TO THINK TIP

Only two numbers are blocked in the top row.

PUZZLE 46
ALPHABET XPLORER 2

Femi particularly enjoys the "Alphabet Xplorer" game on his mobile phone
(see Puzzle 18) because he does well at something he thought he was no good
at. He progresses surprisingly quickly to Level 2. As before, each oval shape
contains a different letter from A to K inclusive. The task is to use the clues
to determine their locations. (When the clues refer to "due" they mean in any
location along the same horizontal or vertical line.)

1   A is due east of H, which is next to and due south of B.
2   A is due south of D, which is next to and due east of E.
3   C is due south of K, which is due west of F, which is further north than H.
4   G is further north than I, further west than H and further south than J.

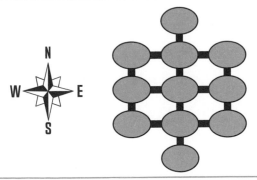

HOW TO
THINK
TIP

A is as far east as you can go.

61

WORK HARDER

5-6 MINUTES

PUZZLE 47
SGT CLEW'S EXAMINATION

Sgt Clew is a cousin of General Drag (see Puzzles 15 and 30), but he works with trainee police officers rather than military cadets. Sgt Clew sets his trainees this test to establish their powers of observation. They need to examine the eight houses shown, establish the pattern of the matrix and work out which of the four boxed designs replaces the one that is missing.

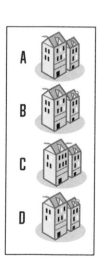

HOW TO THINK TIP

The lights are on.

62

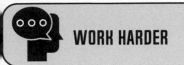
PUZZLE 48
GRANDPA WILSON'S BATTLESHIP 3

Here's a final chance to try your hand at one of the battleship puzzles that Grandpa Wilson devises for his twin grandsons Nile and Nathan (See Puzzles 4 and 19). As the boys have improved their tactical skills, Grandpa has made the puzzles more demanding – and this is the hardest of the lot! As before, the numbers on the side and bottom of the grid indicate occupied squares or groups of consecutive occupied squares in each row or column. Fill up the grid so that it contains three cruisers, three launches and three buoys, and remember that the numbers must make sense. Go on, give Nile and Nathan a hand!

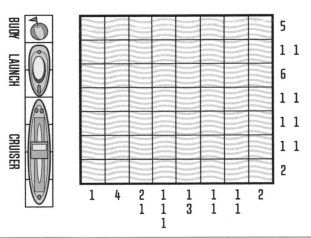

There's a cruiser at the top.

PUZZLE 49
L AND O

Philosophy teacher Ella marketed her game L-O under the title L and O (see Puzzle 12). Here is a trial version she made to present to games manufacturers. As before, there are twelve L-shapes, three of each of the four kinds shown here. They have been inserted in the grid and each L has one O-shaped hole in it. Given the positions of the Os in the diagram, can you tell where the Ls must be? Any piece may be turned or flipped over before being put in the grid. No pieces of the same kind may touch, even at a corner. The pieces fit together so well that you cannot see any spaces between them; only the holes show. Can you solve it?

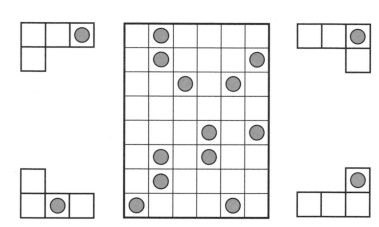

HOW TO THINK TIP

The top-left L is laid horizontally.

PUZZLE 50
SOLO'S SOLITAIRE

Medical student Cristiano Solo moves on from his counter flip (see Puzzle 25) to a solitaire game played with the coins in the ice cream van he drives for his summer job. He uses 14 coins and a 5 x 5 grid: In the usual solitaire style, any coin may jump over any other coin and the jumped-over coin is removed from the board, like in draughts. How can you clear every coin but one from the board? Why don't you try his game? He says, "You get extra credit if you can end up with the final coin in the middle of the board."

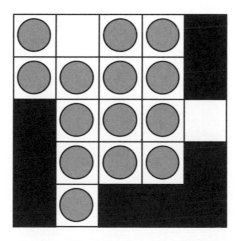

Start by filling the top blank square.

THE CHALLENGE

 THE CHALLENGE **10-15** MINUTES

Now put your tactical-thinking skills into practice as you try to overcome challenges in an almost-real setting. At this level of tactical thinking, it can help to consider thinking challenges like a battle, to imagine yourself as a general surveying the action from a hilltop. You need to be away from the fighting in order to see what's going on. If you get drawn into the battle, you may fight as bravely as you like, but you will be letting your comrades down if there's no one there to make the necessary tactical and strategic decisions and give the orders. Ask yourself, "Do I have an overview? Where am I heading, and how will this response help me get there? Am I maintaining awareness of my ultimate goal?"

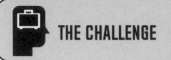
THE RIVER CITY TRADE FAIR

You know what they say about the "best-laid plans"? In this tactical-thinking challenge you have to keep adapting your plans in the face of changing circumstances and competition. You have been dispatched to represent your company at an important trade fair. Not only is the trade fair cancelled, but an old rival – your major competitor – threatens to eclipse you and take over your client list.

You might well be distracted by emotion. If you are dealing with an old rival, you naturally have a strong desire to get the better of him or her. Here it is especially important to ensure that your responses are tactical, aligned with your ultimate goal and realistic. Be careful not to lose sight of the "bigger picture". Ask, "What is my ultimate aim? Will each response I make move me towards this goal?"

Responding to change is a key part of tactical thinking. So try to view the setbacks and challenges as an opportunity to prove your resourcefulness and adaptability. Here your tactics need to be designed to make the best of this difficult situation. If possible, you should aim to maintain your company's visibility and you certainly want to protect, if not build, your client list.

You need to be alert and creative. Be ready to look beyond the obvious. Read through the text three or four times, making notes in the side columns of clues or hints you notice. Try to think of as many possible plans of action as you can. Don't be afraid to head off in unexpected directions – you may need to make creative combinations. Now take a deep breath, clear your mind and read on ...

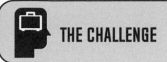

THE CHALLENGE

10-15
MINUTES

You face a major tactical dilemma when your careful preparations for the River City Trade Fair are wrecked.

Here's the background. The small company you work for, In the Bag, manufactures and imports canvas bags. Your boss has sent you to run its stall at the River City Trade Fair, the most important fair of the year for the bag industry. The boss, Fabrizio Baggio, is getting married and has taken the company credit card with him. Your own credit card is maxed out, and you only have £500 cash to pay for all your costs.

On the plane to River City you meet Dave Dibs, an old rival and owner of your major competitor, Bagsy! He corners you and boasts about how he is easily going to outperform you at the fair. You are unsettled by this, but you cheer up when you are welcomed at the airport by your sister, Grace, a struggling artist who lives in River City. She excitedly tells you that the Gospel choir she sings with has just won a national prize and is going to sing at a fundraising party that her husband Will is throwing at their church. And a crew from a music show on national TV is

**NOTES &
CLUES**

THE CHALLENGE

10-15 MINUTES

coming to film them!

Then, on the eve of the conference, at the height of a three-day storm, the trade hall in River City is catastrophically flooded and the fair has to be cancelled. However, the local mayor declares that because so many traders and clients are in town, all rules restricting the setting up of street stalls and displays will be relaxed.

Fortunately your samples and materials are undamaged. You decide to find a new venue, but the flooding is very bad and only one part of the city – on the hill, where your sister's church stands – is free from water.

Your sister says there is only one suitable hall on Riverview Hill – at the end of the road on which her church stands. You try to call the hall, but can't get through, and when you hotfoot over there, the hall manager, Elvis Jones, tells you that the hall will cost £500. You are reluctant to spend all your funds – it will leave you nothing to buy drinks and snacks for clients. While you are there, Dave Dibs rolls up and offers the full amount – he even offers £550. Elvis tells you he will give you the hall since

NOTES & CLUES

70

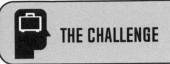
you got there first, but you must pay the full £500. He gives you his number and asks you to text him your decision within ten minutes.

You walk down the road in heavy rain and sit on the church wall. You watch Will and his staff bringing in piles of food for the Gospel choir party.

Then Dave Dibs approaches and offers a seemingly generous deal. Share the hall and the costs, and he will give you a third of profits plus a quarter of new client contacts.

What can you do? Pay the £500? Cut your losses and take Dave Dibs's proposed deal? Try to run a street stall in the rain? What other approaches could you take? What do you do – or rather, how do you think?

NOTES & CLUES

THE ANSWERS

 TACTICAL THINKING PUZZLES

Try to use this answers section as a source of inspiration. We all get stuck sometimes – we feel we're out of ideas and we need help. If you're really stymied, by all means look up the answer to the problem. After reading the solution, try to rehearse the stages of tactical thinking that led to the answer given, so that you pick up the strategy for future use, both with other puzzles in the book and in real life. As with all puzzles, it's possible that you may sometimes find an alternative solution – a sign that you're putting your tactical intelligence to good use.

PUZZLE 1
SYMBOL SIMON

The answers are: circle = 4; cross = 3; pentagon = 6; square = 2; star = 5. Tactical thinking at work or school often requires you to interpret data, and this kind of puzzle is good practice for that form of challenge. The beauty of Simon's game is that once you have solved the problem, you just press Reset on the touch-sensitive screen and the computer in the handheld device generates a new problem with new values for the symbols.

PUZZLE 2
GIOVANNI'S ICE CREAM PUZZLE

The answer is J. The central letter is the value of the total of the two letters on the left side minus the two letters on the right side, so in the final dessert (B + P) – (E + C) equates to (2 + 16) – (5 + 3) = 18 – 8 = 10. The tenth letter of the alphabet is J. Noah got it in 98 seconds and Giovanni gave him a free espresso.

PUZZLE 3
NUMBERCLUSE

The completed grid is shown below. When you're thinking tactically to solve a problem, you often need to process facts accurately and quickly, or follow detailed instructions closely. Exercises like this provide good practice in both of these areas. In the novel, Arthur enters the numbers from the grid in a combination lock on a safe, and in the safe he finds a new clue.

24	25	3	63
46	4	60	15
21	36	12	8
16	1	7	48

PUZZLE 4
GRANDPA WILSON'S BATTLESHIP

The completed grid is shown below. Grandpa Wilson is very proud that Nile and Nathan manage to do it so quickly. "You're just like your Pa", he tells them, "sharp as a tack." Puzzles like these develop your visual logic – which is important for tactical thinking.

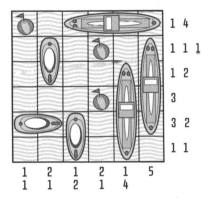

1 4
1 1 1
1 2
3
3 2
1 1

1 2 1 2 1 5
1 1 2 1 4

PUZZLE 5
MATHS MOB T- SHIRT

The correct grid is shown above right with numbers blocked out, as requested by Mr Goldstein. Hasan really earns his money on this job – but luckily he is good at visual logic and tactical thinking and he gets it right. In the end, he and Mr Goldstein decide to print the grid as shown on page 16 on the front of the T-shirts, with the blocked-out version on the back.

4	3	4	2	5	4
2	1	3	1	4	2
4	5	1	4	3	2
4	2	1	5	1	5
5	4	2	1	4	3
1	1	4	3	2	5

PUZZLE 6
NUMBERCROSS

The Numbercross grid is shown correctly completed below. This puzzle requires you to use mathematical logic to do the arithmetic, and visual intelligence to fit the answers in the grid.

4	x	2	−	6	+	1	=	3
−		+		−		+		
1	+	6	x	4	−	2	=	26
x		−		+		x		
2	+	4	−	1	x	6	=	30
+		x		x		−		
6	+	1	x	2	−	4	=	10
=		=		=		=		
12		4		6		14		

PUZZLE 7
BALLOON MOVE

The new arrangement of balloons is shown below. A puzzle like this, which requires logical deduction, provides great practice for many tactical-thinking challenges.

PUZZLE 8
ELLIOTT'S NUMBER GRID

The correct solution to the number grid, as discovered by Morris, is as shown below. This puzzle develops your ability to fit parts logically and coherently into a whole.

3	4	4	4	4	3
1	1	1	1	1	3
1	1	1	1	1	3
2	2	2	4	4	1
2	2	2	4	4	1
2	3	3	4	4	3

PUZZLE 9
THE MATHS HOUSE

There is more than one possible solution. Here is one below, as worked out by Vikram. Brain scientists tell us to work fast with numbers if we want to get our neurons really firing.

12	8	10	8
4	13	11	10
10	7	7	14
12	10	10	6

PUZZLE 10
MR AWESOME'S DEBTS

Mr Awesome owes £50 + £20 and is owed £30, so he must repay £40 to be even. Similarly, Ms Brilliant is owed £40 net (£10 – £50), Mr Charming is owed £20 net (£10 – £30 + £40) and Mrs Dreamy owes £20 net (£20 – £40). Hence, Mr Awesome should give Ms Brilliant £40, and Mrs Dreamy should give £20 to Mr. Charming.

PUZZLE 11
HEXAGON HAVEN

The finished grid, as completed by
Jorge and Diego, is shown below.
All of the adjacent triangles have
matching numbers. Emmanuel tells
his nephews that games like this
develop their ability to weigh up and
evaluate options.

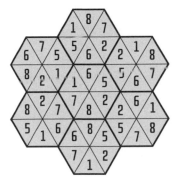

PUZZLE 12
L – O

The outlines of the Ls in the grid
are as shown below. Ella has
developed a version of the game in
which players put 12 L-shapes onto
a board to match a pattern of Os.
She is marketing it under the name
"L and O" and hoping to make her
fortune from brain-trainers and
puzzle fans.

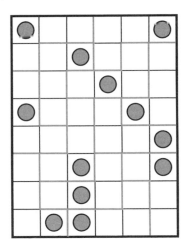

PUZZLE 13
CAP STARS

Edwin should choose C. The correctly completed grid is shown below. Each row and column has one image where two black outlines are visible on the outer circles, one image where the outer thicker line is missing and one image where the inner, thinner line is missing. Each row and column also has two images where there is a ring inside the star, and one where it is missing. Each row and column also has two images with a dot in the middle of the star and one where it is missing. The missing image should therefore have the outer thicker circle but not the inner, thinner one, and both a ring and a dot inside the star.

PUZZLE 14
NUMBER CONNECT

The completed Number Connect grid is shown below. In doing this puzzle quickly, you've stimulated and connected the neurons associated with visual and numerical intelligence.

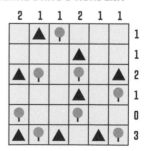

PUZZLE 15
GENERAL DRAG'S ACADEMY

The completed camping ground with tents should look as shown above. The exercised develops

ANSWERS

tactical thinking because the cadets have to proceed logically and laterally, with patience, to find a solution that satisfies a number of rules operating together.

PUZZLE 16
MEL'S CHESS CHALLENGE.

One possible set of moves that covers all of the remaining squares on this part of the board is shown below. "I like it!" chuckles Mel as he watches Marvin solve the problem in just under two minutes. Marvin is an old hand at chess and so is an expert at this kind of predictive visual–spatial tactical thinking.

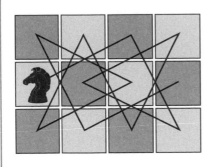

PUZZLE 17
SAM'S SUDOKU

The completed sudoku, as finished by Grace, appears as shown (below). Doing a sudoku really stimulates the brain cells.

6	2	1	3	5	7	4	9	8
7	4	8	1	9	2	5	3	6
3	9	5	8	6	4	2	1	7
1	7	6	5	3	8	9	4	2
2	5	9	4	7	6	3	8	1
8	3	4	9	2	1	7	6	5
5	8	7	6	4	3	1	2	9
9	6	3	2	1	5	8	7	4
4	1	2	7	8	9	6	5	3

PUZZLE 18
ALPHABET XPLORER

The completed grid is shown below. Puzzles like this provide great practice in converting information into schematic diagrams, which can be a very useful skill when plotting relationships between disparate facts in tactical-thinking challenges.

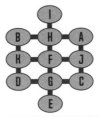

PUZZLE 19
GRANDPA WILSON'S BATTLESHIPS 2

The finished grid, as completed by our junior tacticians Nathan and Nile, is shown right. Grandpa's puzzles give you (and the boys) a chance to stimulate your visual intelligence and to practise holding parallel solutions side by side in your head while weighing up options.

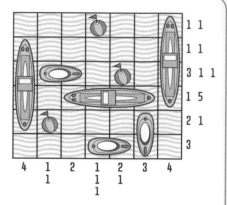

PUZZLE 20
DOMZONE

The completed domino zone game is shown below. This puzzle gives good practice in seeing connections and in the kind of "on your toes" response you often need in tactical thinking.

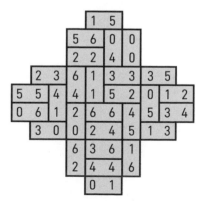

PUZZLE 21
SYMBOL TRANSFER

The completed Symbol Transfer grid is as shown below. This puzzle develops the careful logical thinking that is often a key part of a tactical response to a problem.

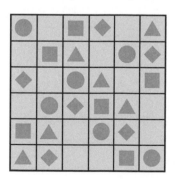

ANSWERS

PUZZLE 22
GRIDBLOCK

The correctly completed Gridblock puzzle will appear as shown below. Tactical thinking often requires you to maintain awareness of complex constraints and rules while visualizing a solution.

PUZZLE 23
THE MATHS HOUSE 2

There is more than one possible solution. Here is the one that Vikram used to get himself across the desert. If he goes wrong, the desert scene dissolves and he finds himself in a torrential downpour on a city street. But if he gets it right, he makes his way safely across the sand dunes.

20	9	12	6
11	9	14	13
5	16	8	18
11	13	13	10

PUZZLE 24
WHAT'S IN JEM'S BOX ?

The value of Jem's Box is 28. The values of the boys' boxes are as follows: Jim = F (13); Joe = E (19); Jack = C (17); Jeff = D (24); Jordan = A (22); Jamal = B (30). The sequence uncovered goes like this: 13 (+6) = 19 (−2) = 17 (+7) = 24 (−2) = 22 (+8) = 30. Thus, the next number must be −2 (30 − 2), so the value of S = 28.

ANSWERS

PUZZLE 25
CRISTIANO'S COUNTER FLIP

The three moves shown below are those needed to turn all the counters so that they show green side up. Cristiano teaches the challenge to his boss, Gianfranco, who has natural visual intelligence. After a little practice to develop his powers of logic, Gianfranco is soon adept at the counter flip and uses it to delight his customers.

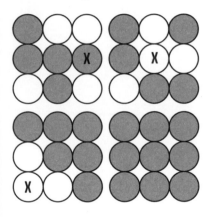

PUZZLE 26
NUMBER CROSS 2

The Numbercross grid is correctly completed below. This intense numerical workout promotes quick thinking and sharpens your mental mathematics skills.

9	–	5	x	7	+	8	=	36
x		x		–		+		
8	–	7	+	5	x	9	=	54
–		–		x		–		
5	+	9	–	8	x	7	=	42
+		+		+		x		
7	x	8	–	9	+	5	=	52
=		=		=		=		
74		34		25		50		

PUZZLE 27
SQUARE DANCE

The new arrangement of squares is shown below. Practical tests of tactical thinking at work or school often require you – as here – to devise new combinations of elements within set constraints.

82

PUZZLE 28
OLGA'S BIRTHDAY CHALLENGE

The completed grid should look as shown below. This was quite a hard task, but as a retired mathematics teacher, Boris did not find it too taxing. Adding a visual-matching element to the challenges of a number puzzle makes this doubly stimulating for your brain.

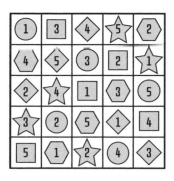

PUZZLE 29
MORRIS'S NUMBER GRID

The correct solution to the number grid, worked out by Elliott, is shown below. The puzzle provides another good test of your tactical nous in plotting information while obeying and balancing rules.

3	1	1	2	2	4
2	4	4	4	4	2
2	4	4	4	4	2
2	4	4	3	3	2
2	4	4	3	3	2
3	1	1	1	1	3

PUZZLE 30 GENERAL DRAG'S ACADEMY 2

The completed camping ground with tents should look as shown right. The puzzle develops your powers of logic and your visual capacity by forcing you to work out the necessary consequences of the listed rules in a two-dimensional display.

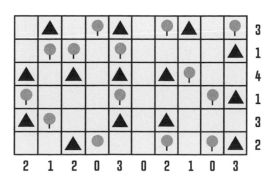

ANSWERS

PUZZLE 31
NUMBER CONNECT 2

The completed Number Connect grid is shown below. This crossword for the highly numerate is great for practising the quick processing and deployment of information.

```
     3 8 4 2 6   4 1 2 2 3 7
 7 6 4   1   8 7 0   8   3
 8   9 8 5 3 3   7 8 1 6 5 9 1
 0   1   7   2 . 7   5   0   4
 7 5 2 2   5 3 0 2 7   1 9 6 5
 3   6   7   4   0   6   5   5
 5 5 7 1 9 0 3   2 3 1 3 8 5 2
         9           4
 4 3 8 3 6 1 9   1 2 6 3 2 0 7
 2   6   4   2   2   3   1   0
 6 9 1 8.   2 6 8 3 9   6 2 0 9
 1   8   1   5   0   7   3   8
 5 0 7 3 5 8 7   8 6 5 3 8   2
     3   7   8 1 7   5   7 4 5
     4 0 5 4 9 6   2 5 3 6 1
```

PUZZLE 32
GREGORY'S CARDTHINK

The cards total 81 (intro), so there is no 10. Card F isn't the Jack, Queen or King (clue 3), and card G isn't the Queen or King. The King isn't H (clue 3 and intro), so the Queen of Spades is H (2), the King is L and the Ace is K. F is the 9 (3) of Clubs (intro). The 4 of Diamonds is J (1), I is the 7 and E is the 5. B and L are Hearts and D is a

Diamond (intro). G is the 6 and B is the 8 (3), so E is a Diamond (1) and G is a Heart. The Jack of Clubs is C (4), D is the 2, and A is the 3. A and K are Spades (intro) and I is a club.

Thus:
3S	8H	JC	2D
5D	9C	6H	QS
7C	4D	AS	KH

Anton worked it out in 2 minutes 38 seconds, but then he's a top card player. How did you do?

PUZZLE 33
DOMZONE DRINKS TRAY

The ten domino outlines should be aligned as shown below. As well as developing your eye for detail, this puzzle gives you practice in holding a number of requirements in balance in your short-term memory.

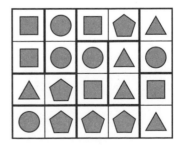

PUZZLE 34
SYMBOL SIMON 2

The answers are: circle = 7; cross = 6; pentagon = 1; square = 9; star = 8. With these values you can see that row 1 is 9 + 8 + 1 + 8 + 9 = 35, while the first column is 9 + 7 + 1 + 6 + 8 = 31. Code-breaking puzzles like this develop lateral as well as logical intelligence, which is critical when you have to "think outside the box" in plotting tactical responses to seemingly impossible challenges.

PUZZLE 35
SYMBOL TRANSFER 2

The completed grid is as shown below. In solving this puzzle, you're like an administrator or general tactically deploying personnel and equipment in locations in line with coded instructions.

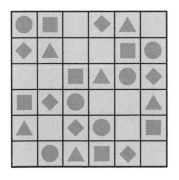

PUZZLE 36
NUMBERCLUSE 2

The completed grid appears as shown below. In this puzzle, the mathematics is simple, the logic more demanding. Nearing the climax of the movie, Arthur solves the number grid and thereby gains access to the address of a crime boss he is investigating.

40	56	7	21
28	3	68	80
12	36	24	16
20	92	4	84

PUZZLE 37
SAM'S SUDOKU 2

The completed sudoku filled in by Grace is below. Doing a sudoku is a great warm-up when you have to complete a piece of work that requires concentrated thinking.

4	3	6	7	8	2	1	5	9
7	2	1	9	4	5	8	3	6
5	9	8	1	3	6	7	4	2
6	1	9	4	2	3	5	8	7
3	5	2	8	7	9	6	1	4
8	7	4	6	5	1	2	9	3
1	6	5	3	9	7	4	2	8
2	8	3	5	6	4	9	7	1
9	4	7	2	1	8	3	6	5

PUZZLE 38
GRIDBLOCK 2

The completed grid appears below. These puzzles develop your ability to maintain sustained concentration.

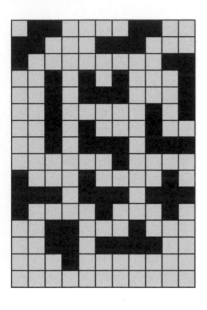

PUZZLE 39
HEXAGON HAVEN 2

The finished grid is as shown below. Emmanuel's pleased to see the boys enjoying these number games because puzzles involving prediction and visualization are really good for the brain. They build connections quickly between neurons.

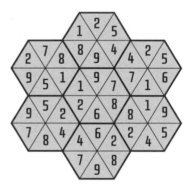

PUZZLE 40
WHAT'S IN BELLE'S BOX?

The value of Belle's Box is 20. The values of the girls' boxes are as follows: Bea = H (9); Bliss = F (27); Bess = B (7); Beth = D (28); Buffy = E (8); Bunty = A (40). The sequence uncovered goes like this: 9 (x3) = 27 (−20) = 7 (x4) = 28 (−20) = 8 (x5) = 40. Thus, the next step must be (40 − 20) = 20.

PUZZLE 41
TURN 2 CONNECT

The final grid, with all the squares connected, appears as shown below. You will see that you can now travel from the top-left to the bottom-right corner of the puzzle. To solve puzzles – and real-life problems – you need a degree of tenacity, but you should try not to stick at things for so long that your concentration begins to fail.

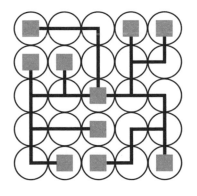

PUZZLE 42
GIOVANNI'S SECOND ICE CREAM PUZZLE

The missing letter is Y. The central letter is the total of the values of all four of the surrounding letters, minus one. Rebecca gets it right, then shares the ice cream with Noah.

PUZZLE 43
BORIS'S BIRTHDAY CHALLENGE

The completed grid is below. Boris and Olga like these number-shape puzzles because they are doubly challenging; both know that really pushing your brain hard stimulates your thinking and keeps you alert.

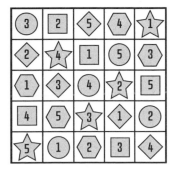

PUZZLE 44
GREGORY'S CARDTHINK 2

The cards total 85 (intro), so the 6 is missing. G is a Heart (clue 1), so E is a Diamond (intro) and the Queen of Diamonds is either B or D (clue 3). If the Queen of Diamonds is D, then the 7 is C and G is the 9 of Hearts (1), which isn't possible (4). So B is the Queen of Diamonds, A is the 7 and F is the 3 of Spades (3), H is a Club (intro), D is a Heart, J is a Heart and L is a Diamond. The 9 of Spades (4) is thus either I or K

(intro). G isn't the 8 (1), so (4) I is the 9 and E is the 8. A and K are Clubs, and C is a Spade (intro). C is the 2 and G is the 4 (1 and 2). K is the Jack (2), L is the King and H is the 5. D is the Ace (1) and J is the 10.

Thus:	7C	QD	2S	AH
	8D	3S	4H	5C
	9S	10H	JC	KD

PUZZLE 45
MATHS MOB MOUSE MAT

The Maths Mob block out the numbers as shown below. Once again, Hasan does a great job, and the mouse mat is a big hit with the students. Hasan even enjoys the challenge, which he finds stimulating, and prepares a version of the number-grid game to share with his teenage son, Muhammed.

1	7	2	9	4	3	2	3	6	8
1	2	7	8	4	9	1	1	9	4
3	8	2	8	5	7	1	4	9	6
6	9	7	2	5	5	7	8	3	3
4	9	5	3	6	1	4	7	8	9
6	4	6	1	5	2	8	1	5	4
8	6	1	5	7	4	4	6	3	5
9	5	4	6	2	8	2	3	1	7
5	8	8	9	9	2	6	2	1	1
5	6	3	5	4	4	9	7	7	2

PUZZLE 46
ALPHABET XPLORER 2

The completed grid of ovals is shown below. This kind of puzzle calls for and develops close reading, logical thinking and a good sense of spatial awareness.

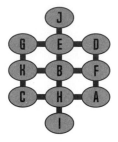

PUZZLE 47
SGT CLEW'S EXAMINATION

The missing house is B. Each row and column contains one image with two lights on, one with three lights on and one with four lights on. Each row and column also has one image with two satellite dishes, one with one satellite dish and one with no satellite dish. Each row and column contains one image with two TV aerials and two images with one TV aerial. Finally, each row and column contains one image where the roof window is missing on the smaller house. The missing image must therefore have three lights on, one satellite dish and one TV aerial, and have the roof window intact.

PUZZLE 48
GRANDPA WILSON'S BATTLESHIPS 3

The completed grid is shown below. Grandpa has watched Nile and Nathan develop their skills in visualization, logic and tactical thinking with these battleship puzzles.

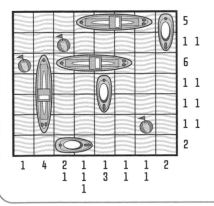

PUZZLE 49
L AND O

The outlines of the Ls in the grid are as shown below. Ella promotes her game by telling manufacturers that it strongly develops visual intelligence and tactical nous by making players visualize possible alignments of the pieces. "Great for vision! Great for Tactics! Great for Thinking!" she tells them. She receives three offers to manufacture the game.

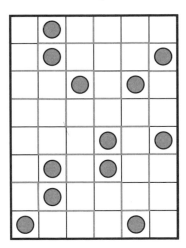

PUZZLE 50
SOLO'S SOLITAIRE

The moves are shown below. The top left illustration shows the board at the start of the game, with the black coin indicating the piece about to move (it reverts to green when in its new position in the following move).

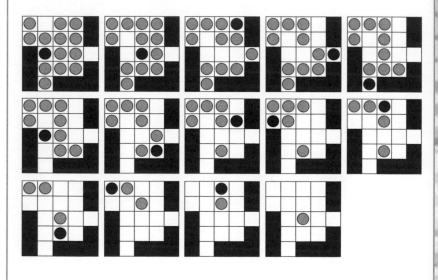

THE CHALLENGE
THE RIVER CITY TRADE FAIR

Dave Dibs is standing staring at you while you try to decide what to do. Your first thought is, "I can't do business with that man". Your second thought is, "But I mustn't let personal antipathy for him get in the way. If this is the best deal for the company, I should go for it. His terms are not too bad. At least that way I would get something from the weekend."

But then you think, "Wait. Let's take a step back, try to get an overview of the situation. Consider what my goals are here. What resources do I have? If I do this, am I using the resources as fully as I can? Can I see a more creative way to deal with this problem?"

Your goal is to attract as many clients as possible. Ideally you want to give them a good time so they are well disposed towards you and In the Bag. If you sink all your money into hiring the hall, you can't buy them drinks or gifts. If you go in with Dave Dibs, you're not going to maximize your client list. The rain is pouring down and it is cold: setting up a stall in the street is unlikely to be a success.

What are your other resources? As you sit there, good smells waft out from the church through the rain. It occurs to you that the Gospel choir concert and the fundraising meal are an attractive proposition. If you didn't have these problems, you'd be looking forward to them. And you remember that a national TV crew is going to be present.

All at once you see a way forward. First, you text Elvis and tell him you won't be needing the hall. Then you tell Dave Dibs "Thanks, but no thanks. You can have the hall yourself." He asks you what you're going to do and laughs at you. He tells you that your boss, Sr Baggio, is going to be furious. You are able to smile back calmly. He goes off, ranting, through the rain to hire the hall.

In the church you have a word with Will. He is happy to help you. You agree that if you donate your £500 to the fundraising total, all your clients can eat for free at the supper and listen to the choir perform. You can display your wares inside the church, out of the rain. And you may even manage to get on TV.

You set to work texting and calling your clients and inviting them to the event. Grace uses her artistic skill to draw up some posters that you mount in the street and outside the church. They say: Come in Outta the Rain! In the Bag presents the prize-winning Riverview Church Gospel Choir with free Storm Weekend Supper. Browse our superb new range of canvas bags in comfort.

Then you go off to collect your business cards and presentation wares from Grace's house and carry them to the church.

In the event, your plan succeeds really well. Not only do ALL your listed clients turn up, but you also get several "walk-ins" from people who were aiming for Dave Dibs's presentation, saw your posters, came in – and stayed.

The choir sing superbly, especially "Go Tell It On the Mountain". The TV coverage features your stall quite prominently. The food includes great salads, pies, chicken and desserts – all washed down with fruit punch and RiverBank Brew, the local River City beer.

You do so well that in the end you are able to make a further contribution to Will's fundraising total. To cap it all, Fabrizio Baggio calls to tell you he saw the event on TV and is delighted with the coverage you have won for the company. Your tactical thinking has paid off.

SUGGESTED READING AND RESOURCES

Aesop – The Complete Fables by Aesop, translated by Olivia Temple, Penguin Classics 2003

The Book of Shadows by Don Paterson, Picador 2005

Brain Rules: 12 Principles for Surviving and Thriving at Work, Home and School by John Medina, Pear Press 2008

The Concise 48 Laws of Power by Robert Greene and Joost Elffers, Profile Books 2002

Daodejing by Laozi, translated by Edmund Ryden, Oxford World Classics 2008

Extraordinary Popular Delusions and the Madness of Crowds by Charles MacKay, Wilder Publications 2008

Fragments by Heraclitus, Penguin Classics 2003

Gandhi the Man by Eknath Easwaran, Nilgiri Press 1997

Here Comes Everybody by Clay Shirky, Allen Lane 2008

Just Enough Anxiety: The Hidden Driver of Business Success by Robert H. Rosen, Portfolio 2008

Made to Stick: Why Some Ideas Take Hold and Others Come Unstuck by Dan Heath & Chip Heath, Arrow Books 2008

Outliers: The Story of Success by Malcolm Gladwell, Allen Lane 2008

Out of the Box by Rob Eastaway, Duncan Baird Publishers 2007

Six Action Shoes by Edward de Bono, Harper Collins 1993

Tactics: The Art and Science of Success by Edward de Bono, Profile Business 2007

The Tiger That Isn't: Seeing Through a World of Numbers by Michael Blastland & Andrew Dilnot, Profile Books Ltd 2008

"To A Mouse, On Turning Her Up In Her Nest With The Plough", poem by Robert Burns in *The Complete Poems and Songs of Robert Burns*, Geddes & Grosset 2008

THE AUTHOR

Charles Phillips is the author of 20 books and a contributor to more than 25 others, including *The Reader's Digest Compendium of Puzzles & Brain Teasers* (2001). Charles has investigated Indian theories of intelligence and consciousness in *Ancient Civilizations* (2005), probed the brain's dreaming mechanism in *My Dream Journal* (2003), and examined how we perceive and respond to colour in his *Colour for Life* (2004). He is also a keen collector of games and puzzles.